Countries Around the World

Afghanistan

Jovanka JoAnn Milivojevic

Heinemann
LIBRARY

Chicago, Illinois

www.heinemannraintree.com
Visit our website to find out more information about Heinemann-Raintree books.

To order:

☎ Phone 888-454-2279

🖥 Visit www.heinemannraintree.com to browse our catalog and order online.

© 2012 Heinemann Library
an imprint of Capstone Global Library, LLC
Chicago, Illinois

Edited by Louise Galpine
Designed by Richard Parker
Original illustrations © Capstone Global Library, Ltd.
Illustrated by ODI
Picture research by Mica Brancic
Originated by © Capstone Global Library, Ltd.
Printed by China Translation and Printing Company

15 14 13 12 11
10 9 8 7 6 5 4 3 2 1

Library of Congress Cataloging-in-Publication Data
Milivojevic, Jovanka JoAnn.
  Afghanistan / Jovanka JoAnn Milivojevic.
    p. cm.—(Countries around the world)
  Includes bibliographical references and index.
  ISBN 978-1-4329-5195-5 (hc)
  ISBN 978-1-4329-5220-4 (pb)
1. Afghanistan—Juvenile literature. I. Title.
  DS351.5.M55 2012
  958.1—dc22   2010038526

Acknowledgments

The author and publisher are grateful to the following for permission to reproduce copyright material: Alamy pp. 18 (© Ulrich Doering), 27 (© Danita Delimont/Phil Borges), 30 (© Picture Contact BV/Ton Koene); AP/Press Association Images p. 11 bottom; AP/Press Association Images pp. 11 top (Haider Shah), 32 (Farzana Wahidy); Corbis pp. 7 (© Diego Azubel/epa), 9 (© Bettmann), 14 (© STR/epa), 29 (© Ahmad Masood/X01429/Reuters), 31 (© David Lees); Getty Images pp. 12 (Flickr/© 2008 Luka Baljkas), 16 (AFP Photo/SHAH Marai), 19, 22, 28 (AFP Photo/Marai Shah), 23 (AFP Photo/Massoud Hossaini), 33 (AFP Photo/Romeo Gacad), 35 (Bloomberg/Adam Dean); iStockphoto p. 15 (© Sun Chan); PA Archive/Press Association Images p. 21; Shutterstock pp. 5 (© Nikm), 13 (© Jon Buder), 20 (© Savenkov), 25 (© Lizette Potgieter), 39 (© Dana Ward), 46 (© Jamaican).

Cover photograph of a man walking down a mountain road, between Herat and Maimana, after Subzak Pass, Afghanistan reproduced with permission of Photolibrary/Robert Harding Travel/Jane Sweeney.

We would like to thank Steve Wright for his invaluable help in the preparation of this book.

Contents

Some words are printed in bold, **like this**. You can find out what they mean by looking in the glossary.

Introducing Afghanistan

Afghanistan has often been in the news in recent years. You've probably seen images of men, women, and children in war-ravaged sites, surrounded by soldiers. Whether they live in big cities or dusty villages, many people in Afghanistan have experienced the horror of war.

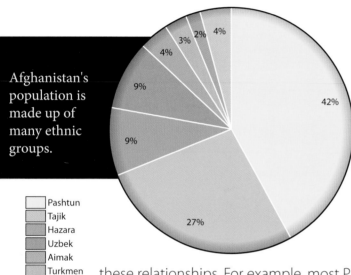

Afghanistan's population is made up of many ethnic groups.

- Pashtun
- Tajik
- Hazara
- Uzbek
- Aimak
- Turkmen
- Baloch
- Other

Afghanistan is located in Asia, just north of Pakistan. Its landscape ranges from rugged mountains to deserts. In the cities, most people live in small apartments, but in the country, houses can be basic mud huts.

Regions and religion

Generally, Afghan people tend to live within their own **ethnic** group. Many villages are organized by these relationships. For example, most Pashtuns live in the south and east, while the Hazara people live in the central portion of the country.

Most Afghans are **Muslims**, people who follow the religion Islam. The rules of Islam say that Muslims should dress modestly, so Afghans wear loose fitting clothing. For formal events, boys and girls may dress in more traditional outfits, such as the *shalwar* and *kameez*, which are a long tunic and loose pants.

Daily life

In Afghanistan, there are regional differences in the **turbans** and hats men wear. Men in one region wrap the turban differently than men in another region. Each style reflects their ethnic group and where they live. In some areas, men, such as President Hamid Karzai, wear woolen caps instead of turbans.

The spectacular mountains in the Badakshan Province of Afghanistan are among the world's highest.

History: Looking Back

Afghanistan's history stretches back some 5,000 years. The Khyber Pass through the Hindu Kush Mountains was once one of the world's most important trade routes. Many different rulers wanted to control the land and the business that crossed through it. Over time, Persians, Greeks, Chinese, Arab, and Indian **empires** would leave their mark on Afghanistan and its people.

Many empires

In the 6th century BCE, the region was part of the Persian Empire. When that empire weakened, it gave a Greek empire led by Alexander the Great a chance to conquer and take control. When Alexander died in 323 BCE, part of his empire fell to the Mauryan Empire of northern India. A few hundred years later, around 50 CE, the Chinese Kushan rulers invaded bringing with them the Buddhist religion.

Arabs entered the region in the 600s, bringing the religion of Islam with them. Later, the Safavid **dynasty** (1501-1722), would **convert** many people to Shi'i Islam. In more recent centuries, Afghanistan would be invaded by other empires. But Islam had already taken a firm hold on the country. It remains the dominant religion today.

GENGHIS KHAN (CA.1162-1227)

Genghis Khan was a Mongol leader from central Asia. He invaded Afghanistan in 1220. His soldiers destroyed many farms and cities. His **descendants** ruled for several more centuries after he died in 1227. Among them was Tamerlane, who developed commerce and made the city of Herat in western Afghanistan into a major cultural center.

This is a statue of Mongol ruler Genghis Khan. He was known as a great but very violent conqueror.

Becoming a nation

In 1747, Afghanistan became a nation under the leadership of Ahmad Shah Durrani. He successfully joined together the Pashtun tribes. As a united group, they were able to throw out rulers from Persia (present-day Iran). But foreign powers still tried to invade and control Afghanistan's government.

Western powers

In the 1800s, the British ruled today's India, Pakistan, and Bangladesh, which were south of Afghanistan. The British waged two wars in Afghanistan, one in 1839 and another in 1878. After the second war, the British took control of much of Afghanistan. Only after a third war ended in 1919 was Afghanistan able to regain its independence.

Changing Afghanistan

In the 1920s, the country entered a period of modernization. Colleges and roads were built, Western medicine was introduced, and women no longer had to wear veils over their faces. Co-ed schools, where both boys and girls attended classes, were also opened. Religiously conservative Afghans were not happy with the changes, however. They overthrew the government in 1928. Some reforms were kept, while others were overturned. For example, women were again required to wear a veil.

MUHAMMAD ZAHIR SHAH (1914–2007)

Muhammad Zahir Shah was born in Kabul in 1914 and became the king of Afghanistan at the young age of 19. He was the last in the 226-year dynasty of Pashtun monarchs to rule Afghanistan. A **democratic constitution** was created in 1964, during his reign. He also encouraged the **Soviet Union** and Afghanistan to become trading partners. He **abdicated** in 1973, but returned to Kabul in 2002, dying there in 2007.

This photo, taken in 1967, shows young women dressed in modern Western clothes.

Modern times

In 1979, the Soviet Union invaded Afghanistan and set up a **communist** government. Millions of people fled to Pakistan as **refugees**. Afghan rebels, Muslim fighters called **mujahidin**, banded together to fight against the communists. The United States believed that the spread of communism would threaten the stability of the world so they supported the *mujahidin's* fight against the Soviet Union. So did a man named Osama Bin Laden.

The Taliban

The Soviet troops withdrew in 1989, but that did not bring peace to Afghanistan. The *mujahidin* rebels now fought with each other in a civil war to see who would assume control of the country. In the meantime, a group of Muslim extremists called the Taliban was formed. At first, people welcomed the Taliban because they fought against corrupt *mujahidin* forces. But the Taliban proved to be cruel. They controlled most of the country by 1997.

Afghanistan has 34 provinces. It's capital is Kabul, located in the northeast of the country.

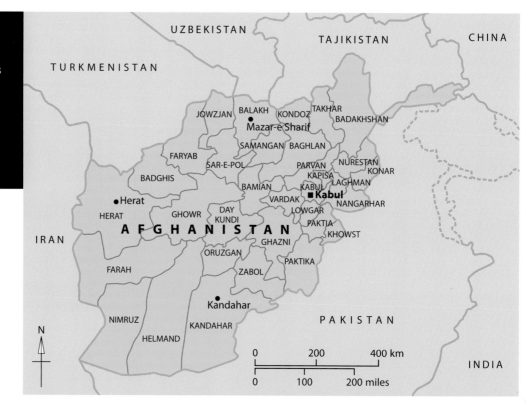

Taliban soldiers get ready to fight U.S. troops.

In 2001, the Taliban refused to give up Osama Bin Laden, who was suspected of being behind the September 11, 2001, **terrorist** attacks in the United States. One month later, the United States led international forces into Afghanistan. The Taliban lost its hold on the country and a new government was established. Hamid Karzai became president. The Afghan people elected him in 2004 and again in 2009.

OSAMA BIN LADEN (1957–2011)

The Taliban gave Osama Bin Laden, who was from Saudi Arabia, a place to train terrorists in Afghanistan. His organization, called *al-Qaeda* (the base), has been responsible for many acts of terrorism around the world. Bin Laden was killed in Pakistan in 2011.

Regions and Resources: Land of Contrasts

Afghanistan is a rugged, dry country. It stretches across 652,230 square kilometers (249,347 square miles) and is about the size of Texas. Iran lies to the west, Pakistan hugs the southern and eastern sides of Afghanistan, and a sliver of China touches its northeastern border. To the north are Turkmenistan, Uzbekistan, and Tajikistan.

Along this northern border is a 1,100-kilometer (700-mile) river called the Amu Darya. A series of rugged mountains extend from the east and level off into **plateaus** along the border with Iran. In the center of the country are highlands, including the Hindu Kush mountain range. The northern plains have the most fertile agricultural soil. The southwestern region is mostly desert. The annual rainfall is low, but melting snow in the mountains provides water for many streams and rivers. This water is used to grow crops.

The Central Highlands mountain range is near Bamyan, Afghanistan.

Climate

Afghanistan is mainly **semi-arid**, but temperatures can vary widely depending on **elevation**. For example, the capital city of Kabul lies at an elevation of 1,800 meters (5,900 feet) above sea level. Kabul winters can be quite cold with heavy snowfall. In contrast, Kandahar, in the south, sits at an elevation of 1,000 meters (3,300 feet) above sea level. It has mild winter temperatures, making it a favorite winter vacation spot for Afghans.

Afghanistan has a large, mountainous desert region.

Daily life

Afghanistan is prone to damaging earthquakes. In July 2010, an earthquake struck Kabul killing 7 people and injuring 30. A devastating earthquake in May 1998 killed more than 4,000 people.

Resources

It has long been known that the northern part of Afghanistan is rich in mineral resources. The Soviets discovered natural gas there in the late 1960s and began **exporting** it. While there have been no significant findings of oil, **geologists** believe there is a great deal of natural gas.

Geologists also believe that Afghanistan has large deposits of iron, copper, cobalt, gold, and industrial metals such as lithium, which is used in making high-tech products including laptop computers. Mining these resources could help expand Afghanistan's economy. But the nation must first develop a mining industry. At present, Afghanistan has neither the equipment nor the expertise to do that.

Another problem is the ongoing war between U.S.-led forces and the Taliban. War makes it difficult for foreign companies to develop the industry. So for now, the resources remain underground.

This Afghan farmer is harvesting wheat at his farm near Kabul, Afghanistan.

The gem *lapis lazuli* has a unique, deep blue color.

Precious rocks

Gems that lie hidden in the rocks of Afghanistan include rubies, jades, and amethysts. More common is the gem stone called *lapis lazuli*, which is found in the Kokcha River valley in Badakhshan, in the northeast of the country. Afghanistan is the world's leading producer of this deep blue stone. It is mostly used to make jewelry.

A young girl begs for money near the war-damaged Darlaman Palace in Kabul.

YOUNG PEOPLE

Afghan street children have difficult lives. Instead of playing or going to school, they must work to earn money for their families. Sometimes, they are the only ones bringing home money. They shine shoes; help people carry groceries; and sell small items like matches, cigarettes, or chewing gum. They can earn maybe $20.00 a month.

Making a living

Recovery after decades of war has been slow but steady. Since the fall of the Taliban in 2001, the economy has shown some improvements, mostly with aid from foreign countries. Afghanistan is a poor country. About 31 percent of the population earns their living through agriculture.

Afghanistan's main export products are dried fruit, nuts, lambskins, cotton, wool, and grain. Carpets and textiles are also exported. About 26 percent of Afghans work in industry and another 43 percent are in **service industries**. Afghanistan's main trading partners are Pakistan, India, Iran, Uzbekistan, Japan, and the United States.

Poppy farming makes a lot of money for farmers, although it is illegal. The poppies are used to make opium, which is then used to make a highly addictive drug called heroin. Poppies grow easily in Afghanistan's dry climate. Afghan farmers who grow poppies instead of traditional crops can double their income. At present, Afghanistan is the world's leading supplier of opium.

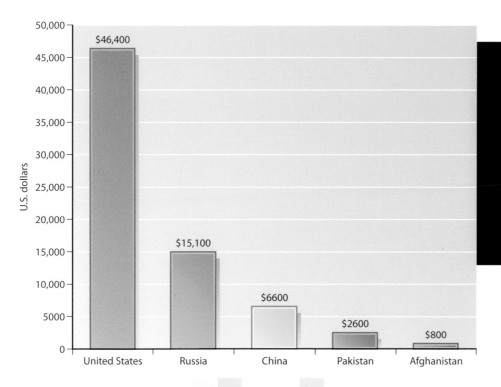

The average worker in Afghanistan makes US $800 a year. The average American worker makes US $46,400.

Wildlife: Issues and Challenges

Few plants grow on most of Afghanistan's dry land. Forests cover some high mountain slopes. At 1,800 meters (6,000 feet), trees such as pine, oak, and wild almond grow. A species of cedar tree called the *deodar* is often used to build homes and furniture. Every spring and summer, flowers such as wild rose bushes and honeysuckle dot the hillsides.

The mountains are home to a wide variety of wild animals. There are wolves, foxes, and striped hyenas. These powerful hyenas have shaggy fur and black stripes and can weigh up to 40 kilograms (90 pounds). Several wild goat species also roam Afghanistan. The markhor has long twisted horns, and the ibex has long horns that curve backwards. Wild cats, elegant gazelles, and brown bears can be found in Afghanistan. Smaller animals include bats, rats, and hedgehogs.

Many varieties of freshwater fish swim in the rivers and lakes. Most can be found on the northern slopes of the Hindu Kush, where the rivers are well stocked with brown trout.

The striped hyena is an endangered species in Afghanistan.

This map shows the elevation and major rivers and mountain range in Afghanistan.

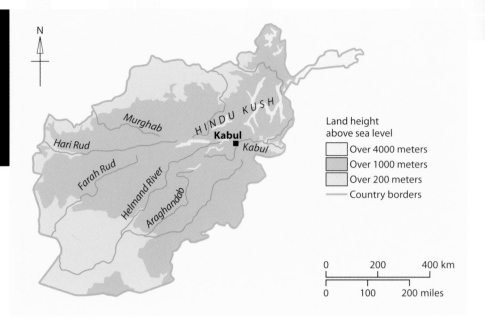

N

Land height above sea level

Over 4000 meters
Over 1000 meters
Over 200 meters
Country borders

Murghab

Hari Rud

Farah Rud

Helmand River

Araghandāb

HINDU KUSH

Kabul
Kabul

| 0 | 200 | 400 km |
| 0 | 100 | 200 miles |

Afghanistan's first national park

Band-i Amir National Park in Bamyan, was established in 2009. The park features six dark blue lakes. People of all ages enjoy swan-shaped paddle boats on the lakes and picnicking along the shore. There is also a motorboat that takes visitors on a tour around one lake.

Visitors enjoy paddle boats at Afghanistan's first national park, *Band-i Amir* in Bamyan.

In the air

Nearly five hundred species of birds have been seen in Afghanistan. Almost half of them live in the country, while others just travel through. The black vulture lives year-round in remote mountainous areas. Some waterbirds spend their winters in the southern parts of the country where it is warmer. Long-legged flamingoes live in the lake area around Ghazni.

Many birds are hunted. Some, such as the Siberian crane, are now considered **endangered**. International wildlife groups are working to help this elegant white crane.

In 2009, Afghanistan's National Environmental Protection Agency (NEPA) released its first protected species list. The list makes it illegal to hunt certain animals, including the snow leopard, the brown bear, and the Paghman salamander.

There is a now an effort in Afghanistan to save the endangered Siberian crane.

Smog

Air pollution has become a serious problem for both people and wildlife in Afghanistan. To stay warm, people sometimes burn trash, tires, and plastics, which release **toxic** fumes into the air. Experts say that the air in Kabul is not safe to breathe. Older cars which burn leaded gas also contribute to air pollution. Finding solutions to the fast-growing problem of air pollution will not be easy.

Thick air pollution clouds the city of Kabul.

YOUNG PEOPLE

The Wildlife Conservation Society (WCS) and the U.S. Agency for International Development provide young Afghans with the tools they need to protect and preserve the environment in the mountainous Wakhan District. The WCS environmental education program prepares young people to interview area residents and keep logs of their findings. The students collect data about wildlife, livestock, forestry, and significant environmental events.

Infrastructure: Making It Work

Afghanistan's official name is the Islamic Republic of Afghanistan. Its constitution separates the government into three branches, although in fact there is little in the way of separation of powers.

The president is the head of the government and is elected by the people. Afghanistan's president must be at least 40 years old and a Muslim. The president has many jobs to do, including serving as commander in chief of the armed forces, appointing important officials, and selecting governors of the provinces. Afghanistan has two vice-presidents.

PRESIDENT HAMID KARZAI (1957–)

Karzai was born in 1957 near Kandahar and is a member of the Popalzai Pashtun ethnic group. His family fled to Pakistan during the 1979 Soviet invasion. Karzai selected several women to serve in his cabinet and appointed the first female governor in Afghanistan's history.

The legislative (or law-making) branch of government is called the National Assembly. It has an upper house, the House of Elders, and a lower house, the House of People. Two thirds of the 102 members of the upper house are appointed by local councils. The president appoints the remaining third, and half of the president's appointments must be women. The 249 members of the lower house are elected by the people.

The judicial branch consists of the supreme court, high courts, and appeal courts. Supreme court judges are appointed by the president but must be approved by the lower house. Once approved, supreme court judges work for 10 years. The laws of Afghanistan must be in line with the basic principles of Islam.

The Afghan parliament is pictured here. Women now play an increasing role in Afghan politics.

The roles (and fashion) of men and women

The roles of men and women in society are greatly influenced by Islam, the country's religion. Traditionally, a woman's role was in the home, tending to children and the household. The role of a husband was, and still is, to provide for his family.

During but also before the Soviet era in the 1970s, women in Afghanistan's larger cities wore Western-style clothing. They attended universities and held jobs. This angered many religious conservatives who rebelled against the Soviets. When the Taliban rose to power in the 1990s, they forbade women and girls from going to school. They believed women should stay home. Women with jobs had to quit. This not only hurt the family's income, but damaged society as a whole. Women were the main healthcare workers and teachers. Without them, the healthcare system struggled.

Women were required to wear a **burka** outside the home. If any skin was showing, even as little as an ankle or wrist, a woman could be beaten on the street by a Taliban enforcer. Men were required to have beards and could be jailed if their beards weren't long enough. The Taliban were defeated with the help of international military forces. Today, women have returned to work. They no longer have to wear the *burka*, and men don't have to grow beards.

Daily life

Divorce is allowed in Afghanistan, but it is rare. A husband can divorce his wife simply by repeating the words "I divorce you" three times. On the other hand, if a woman wants to divorce, she must appear before a judge, who decides whether she can have a divorce or not.

Women in burka shop for carpets in Kabul, Afghanistan.

Education

Traditionally, Islamic **clerics** were the schoolteachers in Afghanistan. They taught reading, writing, and math. But only boys studied the *Qur'an*, Islam's holy book. During the 1980s, the school system expanded with aid from the Soviet Union. At that time, boys and girls attended schools together. But wars and the Taliban ruined much of the educational system.

Today, the country is rebuilding education with help from international aid organizations. Children must attend school from age six to nine. School typically starts at 8 a.m. and lasts until noon. Students study a wide variety of subjects, including math, geography, history, and science. They also learn some English. While parents understand the importance of education, many children are not able to attend school. Sometimes schools are not available in their area, or they must help their families by working. Most high schools are in larger towns and cities.

Under the Taliban, girls over eight years old could not go to school. While girls are now allowed to attend school, people who believe girls should not be educated often harass them. Girls still lag far behind in education compared to boys.

Daily life

The Aschiana Foundation is a U.S.-based non profit agency that helps young Afghan street children get an education. In some cases these children are the main income earners in their families. The foundation gives the family the lost income so the children can go to school.

A young Afghan girl studies for her lessons in a classroom.

YOUNG PEOPLE

Afghanistan has one of the lowest **literacy** rates in the world. More than 11 million Afghans over the age of 15 cannot read or write. In rural areas, where most Afghans live, 90 percent of the women and 60 percent of the men cannot read and write.

Culture: Religion, Art, and Fun

Many different cultures have influenced the art of Afghanistan. Early Indian culture is reflected in some Buddhist art. Sadly, in 2001, the Taliban all but destroyed two 1,500-year-old giant Buddhist statues. But **frescoes** dating back to the 6th century BCE remain. Persian influence can be seen in the tile work from the 15th century CE at the Shrine of Hazrat Ali in Mazar-e Sharif, and in the great works of the 17th-century poet Kushal Khan Khattak.

Music and movies

Today, many people enjoy traditional Afghan music. The influences of India are clear in the instruments and melodies of *qataghani* music. It is nearly impossible not to move to this hypnotic sounding music. *Attan melli* is the traditional dance music of Afghanistan. It is played at weddings and other special events. Dancing is popular at family gatherings. It is said that close friends and relatives should never allow the dance floor to be empty at a wedding. Everyone dances: young people, parents, and grandparents.

Afghan Kochi tribesmen dance the *Attan*, the Afghan national dance.

Some popular forms of music in Afghanistan are not traditional. Many young people like hip-hop music.

Afghan rapper Bezhan Zafarmal, known as DJ Besho, says young Afghans should unite, stay clear of drugs, and study hard.

People across Afghanistan enjoy movies. Movies from India, called Bollywood movies, are very popular. People usually rent DVDs to watch at home, and larger cities have movie theaters. Movies also are broadcast on TV stations.

How to say...

Pashto and Dari are both official languages in Afghanistan. The phrases below are in Dari:

That's cool = *Khobesh*
What's happening? = *Che shoda?*
Hello = *Salaam*
How are you? = *Chetor aste?*

Religion

The teachings of Islam are woven into daily life, culture, and government practices in Afghanistan. Devout Muslims say prayers five times per day. Islam helps unite the various ethnic groups in Afghanistan. There are two main **sects** of Islam: Sunni and Shi'i. Sometimes members of the two sects fight over their religious beliefs. About 90 percent of Afghanistan's people are Sunni Muslims.

Most holidays in Afghanistan are religious. The month of *Ramadan* celebrates the time when Allah ("God" in Arabic), revealed the *Qur'an* to Muhammad, the founder of Islam. During *Ramadan*, Muslims do not eat or drink anything from sunup to sundown. The end of *Ramadan* is observed with *'Id al-Fitr*, a three-day holiday with special foods and lots of joyous celebrations.

'Id al-Adha, another three-day feast, takes place after the annual **pilgrimage** to Mecca, the Muslim holy city in Saudi Arabia. Every Muslim is supposed to do this at least once in their life. Muhammad's birthday and the Islamic New Year are also religious holidays. Islamic holidays follow an Islamic calendar so the dates vary from year to year.

The famous Hazrat 'Ali **Mosque** in Mazari-i Sharif. It is one of the reputed burial places of 'Ali, Muhammmad's cousin and son-in-law.

Daily life

A *muezzin,* like this one, calls Muslims to prayer. Different religions use different signals to call people to prayer and worship. For example, a Christian church might use a bell. Muslims use the human voice. The *muezzin* chants the same words in turn to each of the four directions (east, west, north, and south). Many mosques are replacing the *muezzin* with recorded versions of the call to prayer played over a loudspeaker.

Food and drink

Tea is the most popular drink in Afghanistan. There are teahouses throughout the country where people enjoy tea spiced with **cardamom**. It is served hot and comes in a glass rather than a cup. Sugar cubes sweeten the tea. Sometimes, a person places a sugar cube in his or her mouth and then sips the tea through it. People drink tea at meals and throughout the day.

A woman pours tea, the most popular drink in Afghanistan.

Afghan tea

Try making tea the Afghan way.

Ingredients

- water
- 1 green or black tea bag
- ¼ cup warm milk
- cardamom
- sugar cubes

Instructions

Heat water until boiling. Pour the water over the tea bag and leave in for a few minutes before taking out. Add some warm milk, and shake a little cardamom into the cup. Mix the tea with a spoon. Place a sugar cube in your mouth and sip the tea.

Afghanistan's neighbors, Iran and India, have influenced its food. A bread called *naan* is a staple, along with rice and dairy products. Kebabs are small cubes of meat strung on a skewer and then grilled. A popular rice and vegetable dish is *pilaw*, which often includes carrots, green peas, or spinach. Chicken or meats can also be used. The spices make *pilaw* interesting. Cooks use cumin, cinnamon, and cardamom, or a combination.

Sports

Popular sports in Afghanistan include kite flying and soccer. The most popular spectator sport is *buzkashi*. In this traditional sport, men on horseback try to pick up the body of a headless goat or calf and carry it to a goal, while other players try to steal it away from him.

On a day of cease-fire, Afghan youths fly a kite and celebrate the *'Id al-Fitr* festival, which ends the fasting month of *Ramadan*.

Afghanistan Today

In Afghanistan, young people today have grown up knowing only war and the suffering it causes. The war has left them with many difficult challenges. People do not get the healthcare they need. The educational system also needs a major overhaul. About 90 percent of women cannot read nor write.

Daily life

In Afghanistan, many social customs determine how people should say hello and good-bye.

- Women greeting women: They kiss three kisses on the cheek. At the same time they ask each other about their families and friends. They also say good-bye with three kisses.
- Men greeting men: The same as women plus a hand shake to say hello and good-bye.
- Women greeting men: It is based on how well they know one another. It can be a nod, a handshake, or spoken hello. Kisses are only for family members.
- Male speaking to elder woman: Hold one hand on his chest while speaking to her.
- Youth greeting elders: Boys and girls kiss the hands of the elders, and they get kisses on their heads.

With the assistance of the international community, life is improving. But Afghanistan cannot do it alone. And it should not have to. The country has been invaded and bombed by many outside its borders. Many people from other nations recognize that they have a role to play in Afghanistan. Many have pledged to help rebuild the country.

The road ahead is not an easy one. But with their strength and perseverance, the people of Afghanistan will perhaps soon find themselves in the headlines for their ability to overcome their challenges. Sadly, massive internal corruption is a major barrier to the country's progress.

Twelve million people in Afghanistan now have cell phones.

Fact File

Official name: Islamic Republic of Afghanistan

Form of government: Islamic republic

Head of state and government: President

Capital: Kabul

Largest cities: Kabul, Kandahar, Herat, Mazar-i Sharif

Official languages: Dari, Pashto

Additional locally official languages: Uzbek, Turkmen, Balochi, Kafiri (Nuristani), Pashai, and Pamiri

Official religion: Islam

Population: 28,150,000 (2009 estimated)

Area: 645,807 square kilometers (249,347 square miles)

Bordering countries: Iran, Pakistan, China, Uzbekistan, Tajikistan, Turkmenistan

Lowest point: Amu Darya River, 258 meters (846 feet) above sea level

Highest point: Noshak, 7,690 meters (25,230 feet) above sea level

Natural resources:	Natural gas, petroleum, coal, copper, chromite, talc, barites, sulfur, lead, zinc, iron ore, salt, precious and semiprecious stones
Currency:	Afghani
Poverty rate:	36 percent
Life expectancy:	45 years
Main exports:	Fruit and nuts, carpets, wool, gems
Main imports:	Machinery, food, textiles, oil
Main trading partners:	United States, Pakistan, India, Tajikistan, Germany
Number of radio stations:	48
Number of television stations:	16

Fact File

Famous Afghans: Hamid Karzai, current president of Afghanistan (2010), born 1957 in a village near Kandahar.

Bezhan Zafarmal, Afghan rapper also known as DJ Besho, born in northern Afghanistan in 1982.

Meena Keshwar Kamal, a women's rights advocate who founded the Revolutionary Association of the Women of Afghanistan (RAWA), born in 1956 and assassinated in 1987.

Abdul Ahad Momand, a cosmonaut and the first Afghan to go into space. He spent 9 days aboard the Russian Mir space station. He was born in 1959.

Sultan Mohammad Munadi, journalist who worked for a wide variety of publications including the *New York Times* and the *International Red Crescent*. Born in 1976, he was killed in 2009, when British forces attempted to rescue him from his kidnappers, the Taliban.

Hakim Ludin, jazz percussionist who began his classical career in Germany and now tours and plays with famous musicians worldwide. Born in Kabul in 1955.

Holidays and festivals: **Nonreligious holidays include**:
New Year's Day (March 21)
Revolution Day (April 29)
Worker's Day (May 1)
Independence Day (August 19)

National pride

Article 20 of Afghanistan's constitution says that the National Anthem of Afghanistan must be in the *Pashto* language and that it must contain the phrase *"Allahu Akbar"* (God is Great). Below is the English transliteration.

This land is Afghanistan. It is the pride of every Afghan
The land of peace, the land of the sword. Its sons are all brave
This is the country of every tribe. Land of Baluch, and Uzbeks
Pashtoons, and Hazaras, Turkman and Tajiks with them,
Arabs and Gojars, Pamirian, Nooristanis
Barahawi, and Qizilbash, Also Aimaq, and Pashaye
This Land will shine for ever. Like the sun in the blue sky
In the chest of Asia. It will remain as the heart for ever
We will follow the one God. We all say, Allah is great, we all
say, Allah is great.

Delicious pastries line the counter in this Afghani shop.

Timeline

BCE means "before the common era." When this appears after a date it refers to the number of years before the Christian religion began. BCE dates are always counted backward.

CE means "common era." When this appears after a date, it refers to the time after the Christian religion began.

BCE

3000	Evidence shows an early civilzation and trade in what is now Afghanistan.
522	The Persian Empire begins ruling the region.
329	Alexander the Great and the Greeks overthrows the Persians.

CE

50	Chinese Kushan rulers bring Buddhism to the region.
652	Muslim Arabs introduce Islam to what is now Afghanistan.
1220	The Mongol conqueror Genghis Khan invades the region.
1370–1404	The rule of Tamerlane, descendant of Genghis Khan who developed businesses and established an art center in Herat in western Afghanistan.
1504	Moguls take over Kabul and use it as a military base to invade India.
1747	Afghanistan becomes united under Ahmad Shah Durrani.
1839	The British invade Afghanistan.
1843	Afghanistan becomes independent from Great Britain.
1878	The British invade Afghanistan for a second time.
1919	The British are defeated in a third British-Afghan War. Afghan leaders introduce social and political modernization.
1933	Zahir Shah rules as king of Afghanistan for the next 40 years.

1953	General Mohammed Daud becomes prime minister, introduces social reforms, and establishes friendly relations with the Soviet Union.
1956	Afghanistan and the Soviet Union form close ties.
1959	Laws concerning women are changed. The veil becomes optional, and many women enter college or the workforce.
1979	The Soviet Union invades Afghanistan, and millions of refugees flee to nextdoor Pakistan.
1989	The Soviet Union withdraws its troops from Afghanistan.
1994	The Taliban begin to gain power.
1998	More than four thousand are killed in a severe earthquake.
2001	Al-Qaeda coordinates a series of suicide attacks upon the United States on September 11, 2001.
2001	The Taliban destroy ancient historical statues. The United States and the United Kingdom attack the Taliban, forcing them from power.
2001	UN allied forces, working with the forces of the United Front (UNIFSA), launch air strikes against the Taliban. Taliban forces are ousted from power, but the fighting continues.
2004	Hamid Karzai is elected president.
2006	NATO, a military alliance of countries in Europe and North America, assumes responsibility for security across Afghanistan.
2009	Karzai is reelected president despite charges of corruption.
2010	As of December 14, over 100,000 ISAF (International Security Assistance Force) troops remain in Afghanistan, including 90,000 U.S. troops.

Glossary

abdicate give up power

al-Qaeda network of terrorists who were responsible for the 2001 attack on the World Trade Center in New York City and the Pentagon in Washington, D. C.

BCE means "before the common era." When this appears after a date it refers to the number of years before the Christian religion began. BCE dates are always counted backward.

burka long cloaklike garment that covers a woman from head to toe, including her face

cardamom seeds of a fruit found in Asia that are used as a spice

CE means "common era." When this appears after a date, it refers to the time after the Christian religion began.

cleric religious leader

communist belonging to a system in which all property and goods are owned by everyone and controlled by the government

constitution written document that contains all the governing principles of a state or country

convert bring a person from one belief to another

democratic related to a government system in which people vote for their leaders

descendant offspring of an earlier group

dynasty line of rulers from the same family

elevation height above the level of the sea

empire lands ruled by one country

endangered at some risk of dying out

ethnic race, nationality, or cultural characteristic or association

export send goods to another country for sale

fresco type of painting done on walls and ceilings

geologist scientist who studies the history of Earth

literacy ability to read and write

mosque building where Muslims worship

muezzin man who calls all Muslims to come to their five daily prayers

mujahidin Muslim freedom fighters

Muslim person who follows the religion of Islam

pilgrimage long journey to a religious site

plateau raised flat area of land

province region of a country with its own local government

refugee someone who flees their homeland, usually because of war or natural disaster

sect religious group consisting of members with similar beliefs

semi-arid having light rainfall, typically about 25 to 51 centimeters (10 to 20 inches) per year

service industry area of work in which people perform a service rather than growing food or making products

Soviet Union communist country that stretched from eastern Europe across Asia. It broke apart into Russia and several smaller countries in 1991.

terrorist person who uses violence to try to force change

toxic poisonous

turban piece of thin material wrapped around the head

Find Out More

Books

Alif, Sharifah Enayat. *Cultures of the World: Afghanistan*. New York: Marshall Cavendish, 2006.

Behnke, Alison. *Afghanistan in Pictures*. Minneapolis: Lerner, 2003.

Burgan, Michael. *Countries in Crisis: Afghanistan*. Vero Beach, FL: Rourke Publishing, 2009.

Mortenson, Greg, and David Oliver Relin, adapted for young readers by Sarah L. Thompson. *Three Cups of Tea*. New York: Puffin, 2009.

Stewart, Gail B. *Life Under the Taliban*. San Diego: Lucent, 2005.

Websites

Afghanistan Online
www.afghan-web.com
To find all kinds of information about Afghan culture, history, and geography.

Afghanistan: Hidden Treasures from the National Museum, Kabul
www.nga.gov/exhibitions/2008/afghanistan/index.shtm
Scroll through a timeline to see Afghanistani art through the centuries.

Afghanistan Embassy
www.embassyofafghanistan.org
For information and news from the Afghan government.

Places to Visit

In Afghanistan:
Band e Amir National Park, Bamyan
http://www.wcs.org/new-and-noteworthy/new-park-for-afghanistan.aspx

Kabul Museum, Kabul
National Museum of Afghanistan
http://www.lonelyplanet.com/afghanistan/kabul/sights/museum/kabul-museum

Babur's Gardens, Kabul
The largest public green space in Kabul, recently restored.
http://www.lonelyplanet.com/afghanistan/kabul/sights/garden-park/babur-s-gardens

In other countries:
The British Museum in London will host an exhibition titled Afghanistan: Crossroads of the Ancient World. A collection of treasures from the National Museum of Afghanistan.
http://www.britishmuseum.org/whats_on/future_exhibitions/afghanistan/introduction.aspx

Topic Tools

You can use these topic tools for your school projects. Trace the flag and map on to a sheet of paper, using the thick black outlines to guide you, then colour in your pictures. Make sure you use the right colours for the flag!

Afghanistan had more changes to its national flag in the 20th century than any other country; the colors black, red, and green appeared on most of them. The emblem in the center features a mosque with pulpit and flags and is circled by a border of sheaves of wheat. An Arabic inscription says "God Is Great." At the bottom is a scroll bearing the name Afghanistan. Black symbolizes the past, red is for the blood shed for independence, and green represents hope for the future and prosperity.

Kabul ■

N

Index

[8]